SAM HOUSTON
STANDING FIRM

MARY DODSON WADE
ILLUSTRATIONS BY
JOY FISHER HEIN

1793-1863

~ 2 ~

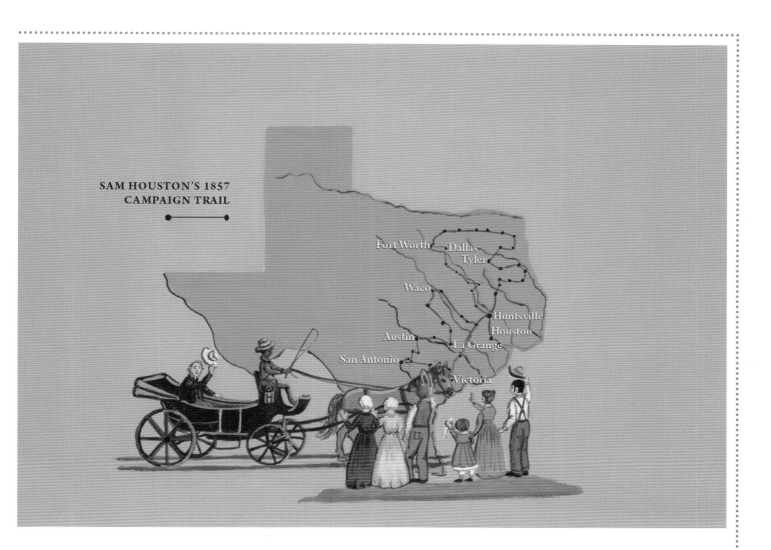

SAM HOUSTON'S 1857 CAMPAIGN TRAIL

Fort Worth
Dallas
Tyler
Waco
Huntsville
Houston
Austin
La Grange
San Antonio
Victoria

HIS OWN WAY

Sam Houston was a big man. He did big things.

He did not always do what other people thought he should. He did what he thought was right. Even when people said he was a bad leader, he did not listen.

Sam Houston worked hard to make Texas a great place.

STUBBORN BOY

Sam Houston was born in Virginia (vir-GIN-yuh) on March 2, 1793. His father died when Sam was thirteen years old. Sam had five brothers and three sisters. His mother moved her large family to Maryville, Tennessee (ten-nuh-SEE).

Sam loved to read. His favorite book was a very old story about heroes. At school, they would not teach what Sam wanted to learn.

He quit.

When Sam was sixteen, his brothers sent him to work in a store. Sam did not like to stay inside. He ran away to live with the Cherokee(CHER-uh-kee) Indians.

Sam was tall. He had blue eyes and brown wavy hair. He did not look like the Cherokee, but he acted like them. He dressed like them. He played their games. Best of all, nobody told him what to do.

Sam even spoke like the Cherokee. For the rest of his life he never said I or me. He just said Houston.

Chief Oo-loo-te-ka took Sam as his son. He gave Sam the Cherokee name for Raven, Co-lon-neh.

TEACHER AND SOLDIER

After three years, Sam went back to Maryville. He became a teacher. He only wanted part of his pay in money. He also asked for corn for his horse. And people brought him cloth. Sam wanted some new shirts.

The next year he joined General Andrew Jackson's army. He was twenty years old. In a battle with the Creek Indians, an arrow hit Sam's leg. He pulled it out and kept fighting. Two bullets hit his shoulder. The doctor said Sam would die before morning.

Sam did not die. Two months later he got home. He looked so bad his mother did not know him.

IMPORTANT MAN IN TENNESSEE

When Sam was twenty-five, he wanted to be a lawyer.
A man told him it would take eighteen months to read all
the law books. Sam read them in six.

Soon he was elected congressman from Tennessee. Next, he
was elected governor. He had a young wife named Eliza, but
she left. Sam would not tell anyone what happened.

Instead, he resigned and went straight to the Cherokee.
They had moved west to Indian Territory. The United States
had promised them food and blankets, but these never came.

Sam's old general, Andrew Jackson, was now president.
Sam dressed like a Cherokee and went with his friends to
Washington. President Jackson remembered his brave soldier.
He gave the Cherokee the things they needed.

COMING TO TEXAS

Three years later President Jackson sent Sam to Texas. He wanted Texas to be part of the United States. Texas belonged to Mexico (MEX-e-koh). Could Sam find out whether Texas would join the United States?

Sam was thirty-nine years old. He liked Texas so much that he stayed.

Texas settlers asked Mexico for better laws. Mexican dictator Santa Anna refused. Texans said they would not be part of Mexico anymore. Sam signed his name to the paper.

Texans knew they must fight Mexico. Sam was head of their army. Santa Anna's army marched to Texas. They killed all the men at the Alamo in San Antonio.

Sam knew his men were not ready for battle. He would not fight right then. Many Texans called him a coward.

Battle of the Alamo   February 23-March 6, 1836

Battle of San Jacinto   April 21, 1836

Finally, his men were ready. The Texans surprised the Mexican army at San Jacinto (san jah-SIN-toh). After a very short battle, Texas was a free country. Sam was a hero.

Texans chose Sam Houston as their first president. He worked hard during the three years he was in office.

After his term as president, Sam took a vacation. In Alabama (al-uh-BAM-uh) he met young Margaret Lea. She was quiet and educated. Sam was much older and very different. His friends thought he should not marry her. They were wrong. Sam and Margaret were very happy together.

TEXAS SENATOR

After Sam had been president one more time, Texas became part of the United States. Sam was elected senator. He was in Washington for thirteen years. Margaret stayed in Huntsville, Texas. She took care of their house and children. Sam wrote long letters to them.

Everyone in Washington knew Sam. He liked to wear different clothes. Sometimes he wore a big Mexican hat. He had a special leopard-skin vest. Sam said that a leopard did not change its spots.

Some states talked about leaving the United States. Sam made long speeches saying that was a bad idea. When he was thinking, he carved toys from wood.

Often Sam's friends did not like the way he voted. Sam wore his vest and did not change his mind.

TEXAS GOVERNOR

Sam was sixty-five years old when Texans elected him governor. A seven-foot bed went into the governor's house in Austin. Rooms were divided so all eight Houston children would fit.

Soon though, Texas decided to leave the United States. The governor had to sign that he would be loyal to a new country. "I will not do it," said Sam. And he wasn't governor anymore.

Sam moved his family back to Huntsville. They rented a house shaped like a steamboat. Indians came to visit him.

On July 26, 1863, Sam Houston died. He was seventy years old. He had helped Texas become a strong state.

IT HAPPENED LATER

Margaret Houston moved to Independence, Texas. Four years later she died of yellow fever. The two oldest daughters took care of the younger children.

Two people were chosen as the most important men in Texas. Artist Elisabet Ney made marble statues of Sam Houston and Stephen F. Austin. The statues are in Washington, D.C. Copies are in the capitol in Austin.

Texas is known all over the world. It got its start with the big dreams and hard work of Sam Houston.

MARY DODSON WADE, a former educator and librarian, is the author of
more than fifty books for children, including *Christopher Columbus, Cinco de Mayo,
I Am Houston, I'm Going to Texas/Yo Voy a Tejas, President's Day,
C.S. Lewis: The Chronicler of Narnia* and *Joan Lowery Nixon: Masterful Mystery Writer.*
She and her husband live in Houston, Texas, and enjoy traveling.

JOY FISHER HEIN is an artist, a gardener and the illustrator of the
award-winning *Miss Ladybird's Wildflowers.* She has been selected as the artist for the
2009 Texas Reading Club. She was also selected by the City of San Antonio
to create thirteen large art panels for Walker Ranch Historic Park.
She and her husband, artist Frank Hein, live in the Texas Hill Country,
where Joy is a Texas Master Naturalist and is certified to create
Schoolyard Habitats for the National Wildlife Federation.

Look for more **Texas Heroes for Young Readers**
to come from Bright Sky Press:

Jane Long: Choosing Texas
David Crockett: Creating a Legend
Stephen F. Austin: Keeping Promises